My book of MAGIC

EUROPEAN LANGUAGE INSTITUTE

Use this secret code to read lots of messages in your Book of Magic.

P.O. Box 6 - Recanati - Italy
Tel. 071/75 07 01 - Fax 071/97 78 51

Devised by J. Olivier, H. Cooper

Illustrated by Giorgio Di Vita

ISBN **88 - 8148 - 221 - 5**

Printed in Italy by Tecnostampa

David, Helen and Peter are ready for a new adventure!
What are they looking at? Colour the dotted areas and find out.
Then use the magic code on page 2 and read the message.

4

Tinker Bell is Peter's best friend. But... which is the real Tinker Bell? Read and find out.

Tinker Bell isn't fat,
she's small and thin. She's got long
hair and she's smiling.
She's wearing a pink dress, a purple crown and a
pair of purple boots. In the picture she's also
wearing gloves. They're purple, of course.

What's
Tinker Bell's
favourite colour?
It's _ _ _ _ _ _,
of course!

Hurry up, Peter! Tinker Bell's flying away.
Follow the clues and join her. Read the message on your way.

A	E	I	A ←	F	N	G
P	S	R	I	M	I	U
N	L	O	X	L	Y	P
G	I	K	E	F	Y	I
R	W	G	E	H	T	N
F	S	E	S	K	Y	J

▼ ◀ ▼ ◀ ▲ ◀ ▼
F A _ _ _ _ _

▼ ▼ ▶ ▶
_ _ _ _

▶ ▲ ▶ ▲ ▲ ▶   ▼ ▼
_ _ _ _ _ _   _ _

▼ ▼   ◀ ◀ ◀   ▼ ▶ ▶
_ _   _ _ _   _ _ _

6

Tinker Bell's very clever. She can do lots of things...but there are some things she can't do! Make sentences using can and can't.

She can sing	She can't play the guitar ....
She can...	She can't... ....
....	....
....	....
....	....
....	....

play tennis

do magic

skateboard

What about you?

	YES	NO		YES	NO
Can you sing?	❏	❏	Can you play tennis?	❏	❏
Can you play the guitar?	❏	❏	Can you do magic?	❏	❏
Can you fly?	❏	❏	Can you skateboard?	❏	❏
Can you skate?	❏	❏	Can you swim?	❏	❏
Can you ride a bicycle?	❏	❏	Can you use a computer?	❏	❏
Can you dance?	❏	❏	Can you cook?	❏	❏

swim

use a computer

cook

ALASKA

The capital of Alaska is Juneau. **Find it on the map.**

There are lots of polar bears in Alaska. They like swimming and eating fish. **Find a polar bear on the map. What colour is it?**

Every year, on the first Saturday in March, there's a famous sledge-dog race. It starts from the city of Anchorage and finishes in the city of Nome. **Find the two cities on the map and draw a line from the start to the finish.**

Caribou live in the mountains. They look like horses but they've got horns on their heads. **Find a caribou on the map. What colour is it?**

Walruses live along the coast. They walk slowly, but they can swim very fast. **Find a walrus on the map.**

Write the names in the grid to find the name of the country next to Alaska.

1. The name of the town where the sledge-dog race starts.
2. An animal which lives along the coast of Alaska.
3. The name of the town where the sledge-dog race finishes.
4. The capital of Alaska.
5. The day of the race.
6. An animal which lives in the mountains in Alaska.

10 Here are Peter, David and Helen during the sledge-dog race. Look at the picture and answer the questions.

1. How many dogs are there? There are six dogs.
2. One of the dogs isn't a husky. Which one? ....
3. There are lots of other animals. Write their names. ....
....
4. How many sledges are there? ....
5. What is the biggest animal? ....
6. What is the smallest animal? ....
7. What colour's Helen's sledge? ....
8. What colour's the glove on the ground? ....

Find the names of the animals in the wordsearch box and read a message.

M	D	O	Y	O	U	L	I	O
O	K	D	O	G	E	S	B	W
U	L	E	D	G	E	D	E	L
S	B	E	A	V	E	R	A	O
E	G	R	A	C	E	S	R	?

__ ___ ____ ______-___ _____ _

12 Match the pictures with the correct sentences and read about Floppy's adventure in Alaska.

Today, there's a sledge-dog race.
Floppy wants to race too.

....

....

....

....

....

❑ Wow! Look at Floppy! He's really fast.

❑ Floppy wins the race.

☒ Today, there's a sledge-dog race.
Floppy wants to race too.

❑ They're off!

❑ Floppy's happy.
He likes his sledge-dog medal.

❑ David and Helen enter Floppy in the race.

Tinker Bell's playing jokes. Look at the icebergs and make comparisons. Use the words below.

Helen's taller than Peter and David.

• bigger • fatter • smaller • shorter • taller • thinner

14  CANADA

Join the dots and then colour the flag. It's the Canadian flag.

You can see sequoias in Canada. A sequoia's a very tall tree. It's the tallest tree in the world. **Find a sequoia on the map and write its name.**

A grizzly's bigger than a polar bear, and it isn't white, it's brown. **Find a grizzly on the map and colour it.**

Ottawa's the capital of Canada. **Find it on the map.**

Find a totem pole near an Indian tent. **Write its name and colour it.**

Belugas look like dolphins, but they're white. Look! There's a beluga in Hudson Bay. **Find it and write its name on the map.**

The Eskimos were the first inhabitants of Canada. Look! This Eskimo's fishing. **Colour his trousers blue and his jacket yellow.**

A beaver's brown and smaller than a bear. **Find it on the map and write its name.**

16

Now the kids are in Canada. Today they're in a park.
What's missing from picture two?

1

2

Floppy,

Everyone's relaxing today. What are they doing?

Floppy	is flying	under the tree
Tinker Bell	is drinking	on a tree trunk
Peter	is sleeping	out of the water
Helen	is eating	on a branch
David	is looking	around the tree
A beluga	is jumping	at the beaver

Floppy is sleeping under the tree.

18  Summer in the forest.

The kids are still in Canada. It's summertime in the forest. It's ......sunny...... .
The leaves on the trees are .... Peter's rowing a ....
on the .... There are two .... in the lake. They're ....
David's looking .... the .... A baby bear's ....
on a .... Everyone's having a great time.

❑ lake ☒ sunny ❑ at ❑ boat ❑ green ❑ beavers
❑ swimming ❑ bears ❑ tree trunk ❑ playing

Winter's cold in Canada. It's snowing, the sky's ....

Peter's .... on the .... David's ....

with a .... There's a lot of .... on the ground.

The .... and the beaver are ....

They're waiting for spring.

❑ lake ☒ snowing ❑ snow ❑ skating ❑ grey
❑ bears ❑ sledge ❑ sleeping ❑ playing

Join the dots and draw the American flag.
It's red, white and blue. Colour it.
Remember that the stars are white.
How many stars are there?

Read these sentences and put the places on the map.

There are a lot of bears in **Yellowstone Park.**

At **Mount Rushmore** you can see the portraits of four presidents.

New York's a city on the Atlantic Ocean. It's also called the Big Apple. You can visit the Statue of Liberty there.

The **Mississippi**'s a very long river. Let's go for a trip on a steamer.

New Orleans's in the south. It's called "the city of Jazz".

Disneyworld's in Florida. You can have fun and meet Mickey Mouse there.

Write the names in the grid and find the capital of the States.

1. The city of the Statue of Liberty.
2. A boat on the Mississippi.
3. A big park.
4. The mountain with the presidents.
5. A very long river.
6. The city of Jazz.
7. The symbol of the States.
8. New York is on the .... coast.
9. Meet famous actors here.
10. It's in Florida.

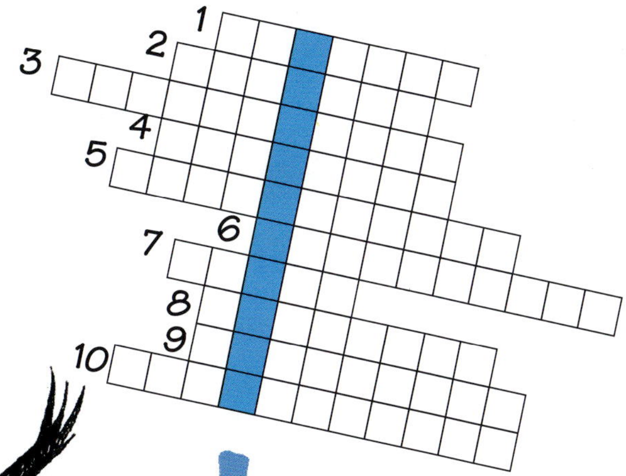

22 The kids are in the United States for a week.
There are lots of interesting places to visit.

Look at page 22and make sentences.

On Monday they're going to New York to visit the Statue of Liberty.

On .... they're going to .... to see ....

On .... they're .... to ....

.... they .... to ....

....

....

....

24  Where are they going? Read the message and find out.

______! __'__ _____ __ ___ _______.

It's Carnival time. Everyone's having fun.

Look at the picture on page 25 and answer true or false.

		T	F
1.	Peter's playing the trumpet.	☒	❑
2.	Three people are playing the trumpet.	❑	❑
3.	Nobody's playing the guitar.	❑	❑
4.	Floppy's near David.	❑	❑
5.	Helen's playing the drum.	❑	❑
6.	It's snowing.	❑	❑
7.	There are seven instruments.	❑	❑
8.	Floppy's running.	❑	❑

This is a great place to visit.

The girls in Disneyworld are very pretty. What are their names? Read and find out.

Paula's at the front.

Liz's at the back.

Jenny's behind Paula and in front of **Lucy**.

Sheila's in front of Liz.

Claire's between Sheila and **Ann**.

Geena's between Ann and Lucy.

IT'S REALLYGREAT.
WHATABOUTARIDEONTHEROLLERCOASTER?
DON'T BE AFRAID
Read the message on the Roller-coaster
5
4
3
2
1
PAULA

Did you like Disneyworld? Look at the picture on pages 26 and 27 again. Then answer true or false.

		T	F
1.	Helen's got a blue flag.	☒	☐
2.	David's wearing a funny hat.	☐	☐
3.	There are twelve girls.	☐	☐
4.	The girls are wearing red and white hats.	☐	☐
5.	There are three cars on the Roller-coaster.	☐	☐
6.	The cars are all red.	☐	☐
7.	Floppy's running to the Roller-coaster.	☐	☐
8.	There's an aeroplane in the sky.	☐	☐
9.	Peter's getting on the Roller-coaster.	☐	☐
10.	Tinker Bell's talking to Mickey Mouse.	☐	☐

Do you remember?

What's the name of the girl at the back?

....

Pancakes are very popular for breakfast in the United States. Here's how to make them.

You need:

JAMAICA

Join the dots and complete the Jamaican flag. Then colour it.

You can swim and touch the

_ _ _ _ _ _ _ _

in Montego Bay.

Write the names in the grid and find the name of the capital of Jamaica.

1. Jamaica is in the ... sea.
2. You can touch the ... in Montego Bay.
3. The man in the picture is playing a ... .
4. Jamaica is an ... .
5. Look at the picture. There's a palm... .
6. The colour of the sand in Jamaica is ... .
7. The people who live in Jamaica are called ... .

The kids are in Jamaica. It's very, very hot.

Look at the picture and answer the questions.

1. Where are the kids?
   They're at the beach.
2. Is there a palm tree on the beach?
   ...
3. What colour's David's swimming costume?
   ...
4. What colour's Helen's swimming costume?
   ...
5. What's Peter doing?
   ...
6. What's Floppy doing?
   ...
7. Where's Tinker Bell?
   ...
8. Is Helen eating a banana?
   ...
9. What's the weather like?
   ...
10. Is there a dolphin in the water?
   ...

AUSTRALIA

Complete this fact file of Australia with the words below:

16,506,000

Aborigines

English

7,686,848 sq km

Australian dollar

First inhabitants:

Area:

Population:

Language:

Currency:

Flag

Look! A young Aborigine is throwing his boomerang.
Where does it go? Read the descriptions and follow it.
The letters in the boxes spell the capital of Australia.

It's a city in the centre of Australia.

It looks like a dog. What is it?

Look out! There's a very dangerous animal.

It lives in the water but it isn't a fish.

It's a very colourful bird.

This sport is popular in Australia, and it's great fun, too!

Swimming underwater is very exciting. There are lots of beautiful things to see.

It doesn't run, it jumps.

C							

36  Helen's talking to Tommy. He's an Aborigine. Helen's very curious and wants to know lots of things. Complete the dialogue and match the balloons.

What 's your name?	Yes, I am.
.... you Australian?	I'm eleven years old.
.... do you live?	My name's Tommy.
.... old are you?	I live in Alice Springs. It's in the centre of Australia.
.... you like Australian animals?	Yes, of course. I love dancing and playing music.
.... you got any special hobbies?	Yes, I do. My favourite's the crocodile.

- ☐ How
- ☐ Are
- ☐ Have
- ☒ What
- ☐ Do
- ☐ Where

Help Tinker Bell join the kangaroo. Read the message on your way.

O	B	A	S	I	N	T
R	I	N	A	D	O	U
I	G	E	A	I	D	N
N	E	M	N	S	E	R
O	W	T	P	A	T	S
R	D	I	G	N	D	A

▼ ◀ ▼ ◀ ▲ ◀ ◀ ▼ ▶ ▼ ◀ ▼ ▶

I S _ _ _ _ _ _ _ _ _ _ _

▼ ◀ ▼ ▶ ▶ ▲ ▲ ▲ ▶ ▼ ▶

_ _ _ _ . _ _ _ _ _ _ _ :

“▲ ▲ ▶ ▲’ ▶

_ _ _ _ _

▼ ▼ ◀ ▼ ▶ ▼ ◀ ◀ ▼ ▶”

_ _ _ _ _ _ _ _ _ _.

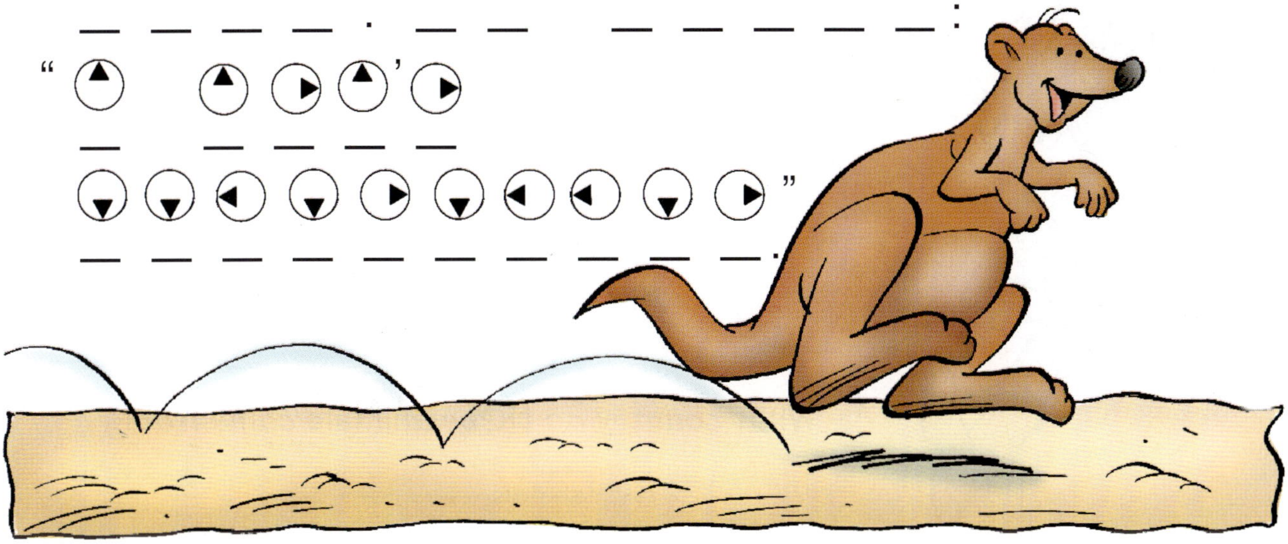

38  There are lots of animals on this page. Help Peter to find them.

two dingoes ....

....

....

....

What country do these animals come from?

They come from ....

Helen likes taking photographs...but, oh dear!
She isn't a good photographer.
Can you guess the name of each animal?

Which animal is it? Write the number of the picture in the box.

This animal looks like a dog but it's much bigger and much more dangerous.	3
It's a bird. It's really beautiful and very colourful.	
It can jump very far and has got a long tail.	
Don't go swimming near it. This animal's got a very big mouth. It's dangerous!	
This animal's lovely, but very shy. It lives and sleeps in the trees.	

NEW ZEALAND

The kids are flying to New Zealand.
Read the sentences and number the pictures on the map.

1. New Zealand's in the Pacific Ocean, south-east of Australia. The original inhabitants are called **Maoris.** They like dancing and have a traditional dance called the Haka.

2. There are lots of **kiwis** in New Zealand. Kiwis are fruit but did you know that they're also birds? Very big brown birds!

3. The **royal albatross** is a very big bird. There are lots of them in New Zealand. What colour is it?

4. There are lots of **sheep** on the islands.

Read the message.

OURTRIPAROUNDTHEWORLDISOVER.WEENJOYEDITVERYMUCH.WHATABOUTYOU?

Find these words in the wordsearch box. The remaining letters spell the name of the capital of New Zealand.

- ☒ Maoris
- ❑ sheep
- ❑ albatross
- ❑ big
- ❑ dance
- ❑ island
- ❑ Pacific
- ❑ bird
- ❑ kiwi
- ❑ haka
- ❑ fruit
- ❑ Ocean
- ❑ white
- ❑ kids

A	W	I	S	L	A	N	D	W
L	P	A	C	I	F	I	C	H
B	B	D	B	K	H	F	O	I
A	I	A	I	I	A	R	C	T
T	G	N	R	W	K	U	E	E
R	E	C	D	I	A	I	A	K
O	L	E	L	I	N	T	N	I
S	G	M	A	O	R	I	S	D
S	H	E	E	P	T	O	N	S

Do you want to go on a trip around the world too? Take a dice and go to START!

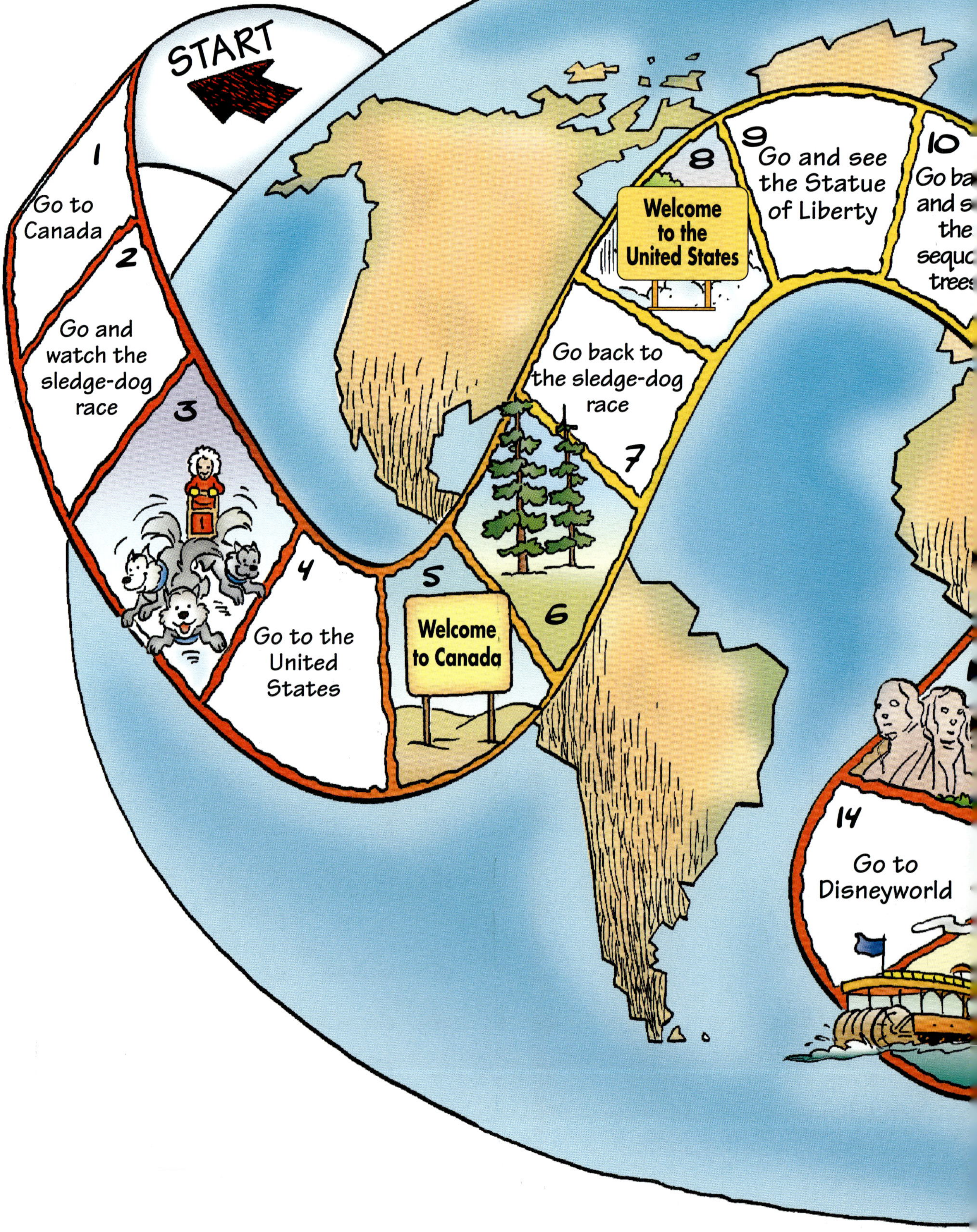

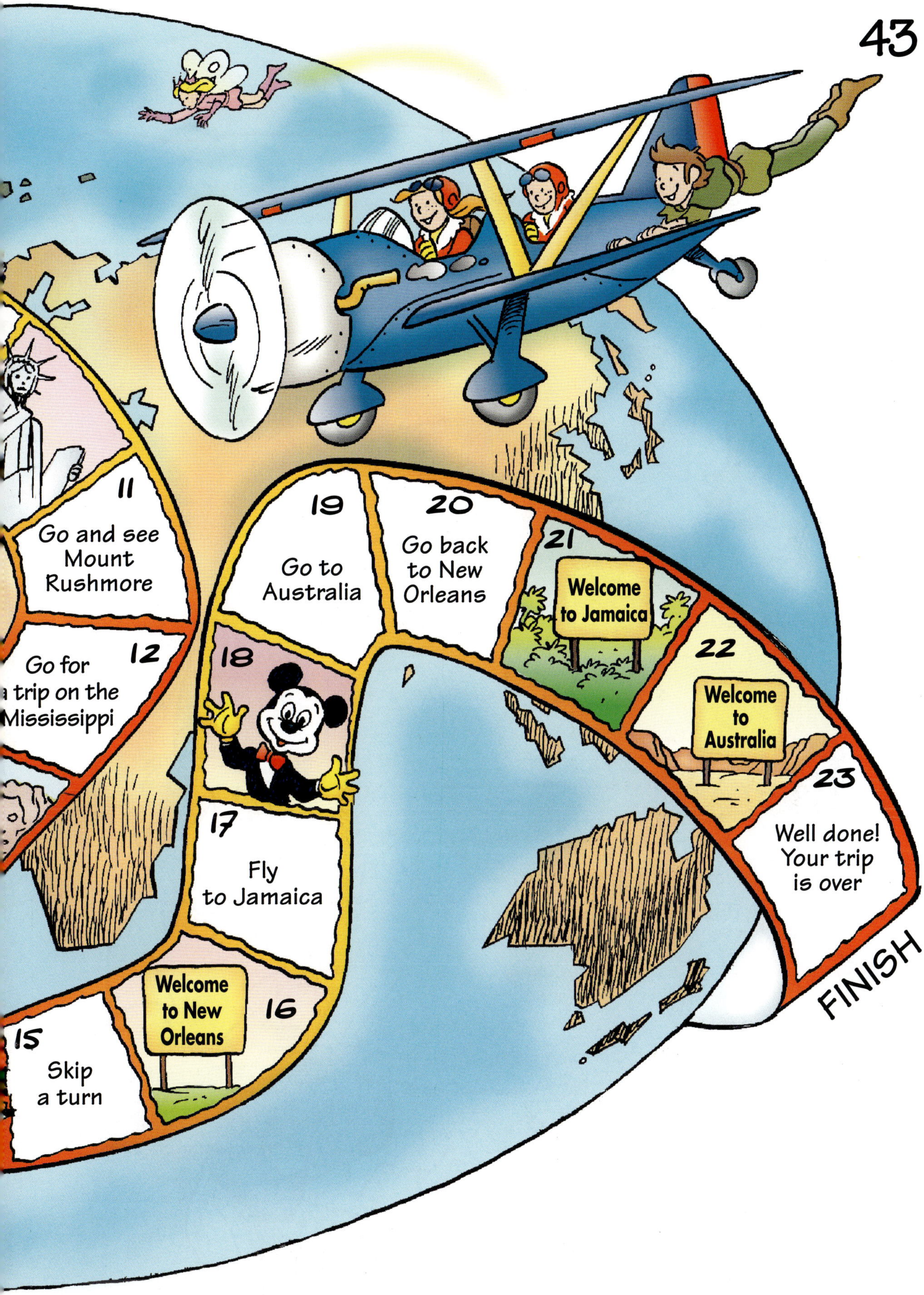
11
Go and see Mount Rushmore
12
Go for a trip on the Mississippi
15
Skip a turn
16
Welcome to New Orleans
17
Fly to Jamaica
18
19
Go to Australia
20
Go back to New Orleans
21
Welcome to Jamaica
22
Welcome to Australia
23
Well done! Your trip is over
FINISH

**Now our magic adventure is over.
We enjoyed it very much. Did you?**

What country did you like the best? ....

What was your favourite animal? ....

Who was your favourite character? ....

Page 3

Hello! I'm Tinker Bell. Let's do Magic together!

Page 4

The real Tinker Bell is number 5.
Tinker Bell's favourite colour is purple, of course!

Page 5

Fairies like flying up in the sky.

Page 6

She can sing.	*She can't play the guitar.*
She can fly.	*She can't play tennis.*
She can dance.	*She can't ride a bicycle.*
She can do magic.	*She can't skate.*
She can skateboard.	*She can't use a computer.*
She can swim.	*She can't cook.*

Page 9

1.An**c**horage, 2.w**a**lrus, 3.**N**ome, 4.June**a**u,
5.Satur**d**ay, 6.c**a**ribou: **Canada**.

Pages 10/11

1. There are six dogs.
2. Floppy isn't a husky.
3. Owl, mouse, bear, beaver.
4. There are three sledges.
5. The bear's the biggest animal.
6. The mouse's the smallest animal.
7. Helen's sledge is red.
8. It's yellow.

Do you like sledge-dog races?

Page 12

1. Today, there's a sledge-dog race.
   Floppy wants to race too.
2. David and Helen enter Floppy in the race.
3. They're off!
4. Wow! Look at Floppy! He's really fast.
5. Floppy wins the race.
6. Floppy's happy.
   He likes his sledge-dog medal.

Page 13

Helen's taller than Peter and David.
Peter and David are shorter than Helen.
Peter's shorter than David.
David's thinner than Peter.
Peter's fatter than David.
Helen's thinner than David and Peter.
Floppy's bigger than the husky.
The husky's smaller than Floppy.
(You can make more sentences!)

Page 16

Floppy, a beaver, two sequoias, a bear.

Page 17

1. Floppy is sleeping under the tree.
2. Tinker Bell is flying around the tree.
3. Peter is drinking on a branch.
4. Helen is looking at the beaver.
5. David is eating on a tree trunk.
6. A beluga is jumping out of the water.

Page 18

The kids are still in Canada. It's summertime in the forest.

It's *sunny*. The leaves on the trees are *green* . Peter's rowing a *boat* on the *lake*. There are two *beavers* in the lake. They're *swimming*. David's looking *at* the *bears*. A baby bear's *playing* on a *tree trunk* . Everyone's having a great time.

Page 19

Winter's cold in Canada. It's *snowing,* the sky's *grey*. Peter's *skating* on the *lake*. David's *playing* with a *sledge* . There's a lot of *snow* on the ground. The *bears* and the beaver are *sleeping*. They're waiting for spring.

Pages 20/21

There are fifty stars.
1.Ne**w** York, 2.ste**a**mer, 3.Yellow**s**tone, 4.Rus**h**more, 5.Missi**i**ssippi, 6.**N**ew Orleans, 7.Ea**g**le, 8.A**t**lantic, 9.H**o**llywood, 10.Dis**n**eyworld: ***Washington.***

Pages 22/23

On Monday they're going to New York to visit the Statue of Liberty.
On Tuesday they're going to Mount Rushmore to see the portraits of the presidents.
On Wednesday they're going to Hollywood to meet their favourite actors.
On Thursday they're going to Yellowstone to see the bears.
On Friday they're going to the Mississippi to go on a steamer.
On Saturday they're going to New Orleans to see the carnival.
On Sunday they are going to Disneyworld to have fun.

Page 24

Hurray! We're going to New Orleans.
1.true, 2.false, 3.false, 4.false, 5.true, 6.false, 7.false, 8.true.

Pages 26/27

Welcome to Disneyworld.
What about a ride on the Roller-coaster? Don't be afraid, it's really great!
1.Paula, 2.Jenny, 3.Lucy, 4.Geena, 5.Ann, 6.Claire, 7.Sheila, 8.Liz.

Page 28

1.true, 2.true, 3.false, 4.true, 5.true, 6.false, 7.false, 8.true, 9.false, 10.false.
Her name's Liz.

Pages 30/31

1.Car**i**bbean, 2.dolphi**n**s, 3.**g**uitar, 4.i**s**land, 5.**t**ree, 6.yell**o**w, 7.Jamaica**n**s: ***Kingston***

Pages 32/33

1. They're at the beach.
2. Yes, there is.
3. It's red.
4. It's pink.
5. He's buying some fruit.
6. He's swimming.
7. She's in front of Floppy.
8. No, she isn't.
9. It's sunny.
10. No, there isn't.

Page 34

First inhabitants:	Aborigines
Area:	7,686,848 sq km
Population:	16,506,000
Language:	English
Currency:	Australian dollar

Canberra is the capital of Australia.

Page 36

What's your name?
My name's Tommy.
Are you Australian?
Yes, I am.
Where do you live?
I live in Alice Springs....
How old are you?
I'm eleven years old.
Do you like Australian animals?
Yes, I do. My favourite's the crocodile.
Have you got any special hobbies?
Yes, of course. I love dancing...

Page 37

... is an Aborigine word. It means "I don't understand".

Pages 38

Two dingoes, four koalas, three kangaroos, five crocodiles.
They come from Australia.

Page 39

1.crocodile, 2.koala bear, 3.dingo, 4.kangaroo, 5.lyrebird.
3-5-4-1-2

Page 41

The **royal albatross** is white.
Wellington is the capital of New Zealand.